THE SECRET RECIPE BOOK

BY: _______________________

Table of Contents

Recipe   Page

Recipe

Page

Recipe   Page

Recipe

Servings _______ Prep Time _______

Amt Ingredient

Instructions

Recipe

Servings

Amt

Prep Time

Ingredient

Instructions

Recipe

Servings

Prep Time

Amt

Ingredient

Instructions

Recipe

Servings _____ Prep Time _____

Amt Ingredient

Instructions

Recipe

Servings _______   Prep Time _______

Amt   Ingredient

Instructions

Recipe

Servings ___________ **Prep Time** ___________

Amt	Ingredient

Instructions

Recipe

Servings _______ **Prep Time** _______

Amt	Ingredient

Instructions

Recipe

Servings ___________   Prep Time ___________

Amt   Ingredient

Instructions

Recipe

Servings ______ **Prep Time** ______

Amt	Ingredient

Instructions

Recipe

Servings ______   Prep Time ______

Amt   Ingredient

Instructions

Recipe

Servings _______ Prep Time _______

Amt   Ingredient

Instructions

Recipe

Servings _______ Prep Time _______

Amt   Ingredient

Instructions

Recipe

Servings _______ **Prep Time** _______

Amt	Ingredient

Instructions

Recipe

Servings _______ Prep Time _______

Amt   Ingredient

Instructions

Recipe _______________

Servings _______________ Prep Time _______________

Amt Ingredient

Instructions

Recipe

Servings _______ Prep Time _______

Amt   Ingredient

Instructions

Recipe

Servings ___________ Prep Time ___________

Amt Ingredient

Instructions

Recipe

Servings __________   Prep Time __________

Amt   Ingredient

Instructions

Recipe

Servings _______ **Prep Time** _______

Amt	Ingredient

Instructions

Recipe

Servings ___________   Prep Time ___________

Amt	Ingredient

Instructions

Recipe

Servings   Prep Time

Amt   Ingredient

Instructions

Recipe

Servings ___________ Prep Time ___________

Amt   Ingredient

Instructions

Recipe

Servings _____ Prep Time _____

Amt | Ingredient

Instructions

Recipe

Servings _____ Prep Time _____

Amt Ingredient

Instructions

Recipe

Servings ____ Prep Time ____

Amt Ingredient

Instructions

Recipe

Servings ___________   Prep Time ___________

Amt   Ingredient

Instructions

Recipe

Servings _____ Prep Time _____

Amt   Ingredient

Instructions

Recipe

Servings _______   **Prep Time** _______

Amt	Ingredient

Instructions

Recipe

Servings ______ **Prep Time** ______

Amt	Ingredient

Instructions

Recipe

Servings ____ Prep Time ____

Amt — Ingredient

Instructions

Recipe

Servings ______   **Prep Time** ______

Amt	Ingredient

Instructions

Recipe

Servings _______   Prep Time _______

Amt   Ingredient

Instructions

Recipe

Servings _____ Prep Time _____

Amt · Ingredient

Instructions

Recipe

Servings ___________ Prep Time ___________

Amt Ingredient

Instructions

Recipe

Servings _______________ Prep Time _______________

Amt Ingredient

Instructions

RECIPE

SERVINGS

PREP TIME

AMT

INGREDIENT

Instructions

Recipe

Servings _______ Prep Time _______

Amt	Ingredient

Instructions

RECIPE

SERVINGS _______ PREP TIME _______

AMT INGREDIENT

Instructions

Recipe

Servings ________ Prep Time ________

Amt Ingredient

Instructions

RECIPE

SERVINGS   PREP TIME

AMT   INGREDIENT

Instructions

Recipe

Servings _______ **Prep Time** _______

Amt	Ingredient

Instructions

Recipe

Servings _______ **Prep Time** _______

Amt	Ingredient

Instructions

Recipe

Servings _______ **Prep Time** _______

Amt	Ingredient

Instructions

Recipe

Servings ___________ Prep Time ___________

Amt Ingredient

Instructions

Recipe

Servings _______ Prep Time _______

Amt   Ingredient

Instructions

Recipe

Servings _______ **Prep Time** _______

Amt	Ingredient

Instructions

Recipe

Servings _______ **Prep Time** _______

Amt	Ingredient

Instructions

RECIPE

SERVINGS _______ PREP TIME _______

AMT   INGREDIENT

Instructions